EARTH DAY

A TRUE BOOK®

by

Nancy I. Sanders

Children's Press®

A Division of Scholastic Inc.

New York Toronto London Auckland Sydney
Mexico City New Delhi Hong Kong
Danbury, Connecticut

Schoolchildren making speeches at an Earth Day event

Reading Consultant
Jeanne Clidas, Ph.D.
National Reading Consultant and Professor of Reading, SUNY Brockport

Dedication
For Beth and David Layton and cherished memories of our home in Black Valley.

Library of Congress Cataloging-in-Publication Data

Sanders, Nancy I.
    Earth Day / by Nancy I. Sanders.
        p. cm. — (A true book)
    Includes bibliographical references and index.
    Contents: Honoring our planet — Our planet, our home —The birth of Earth Day — Let's keep it clean! — One world, one voice — Earth Day every day.
    ISBN 0-516-22762-9 (lib. bdg.) 0-516-27776-6 (pbk.)
    1. Earth Day—Juvenile literature. 2. Environmentalism—Juvenile literature. 3. Environmental protection—Juvenile literature. [1. Earth Day. 2. Environmental protection. 3. Holidays.] I. Title. II. Series.
GE195.5.S36 2003
333.7'2—dc21

2003004515

CHILDREN'S PRESS, and A TRUE BOOK®, and associated logos are trademarks and or registered trademarks of Scholastic Library Publishing. SCHOLASTIC and associated logos are trademarks and or registered trademarks of Scholastic Inc.

1 2 3 4 5 6 7 8 9 10 R 12 11 10 09 08 07 06 05 04 03

Contents

Honoring Our Planet

Look outside. Do you see fluffy white clouds floating across the sky? Do you see birds singing in a nearby tree? Do you see green grass and brightly colored flowers? The Earth has all these wonderful things— and more!

On Earth Day, people spread the word about taking care of our planet.

Earth is the planet on which we live. We share this special home with many different plants and animals. Every spring, people all around the

6

world join together to honor our planet. This holiday, celebrated on April 22, is called Earth Day.

Schools play an important part in the celebration of Earth Day. Teachers help children learn important lessons about keeping the Earth clean and healthy. Students are taught about recycling—using trash to make new things. They learn how to save **natural resources** such as water and trees. Schools are working

Earth Day activities include learning about recycling (left) and planting trees (above).

hard to encourage children and their families to learn how to help the Earth today, as well as in years to come.

Why We Need Earth Day

In the late 1700s, great changes were taking place in the world. New machines were invented that made products or did certain jobs more quickly and easily. Factories were built and **industries** were established. This new way of producing

Factories produce things quickly and easily, but the fuel burned to run them creates lots of pollution.

goods came to be called the Industrial Revolution.

In the 1800s and 1900s, the Industrial Revolution started to affect our planet. Over the years, industries used a lot of wood, coal, and oil for fuel. These natural resources take millions of years to develop in the ground. The factories began using them up faster than the natural resources could form.

Industries also created a lot of pollution. Smokestacks sent black clouds of smoke up into the air. Dirty water filled with harmful chemicals traveled through pipes from the factories to rivers and streams. The polluted water then ran into the oceans.

Pollution was hurting the Earth. The water in some rivers and lakes became so polluted that fish died and children couldn't swim in them. Smog, a dirty mixture of smoke and fog, filled the sky in some cities. Rain containing dangerous chemicals, called acid rain, hurt the trees and plants on which it fell. So much trash was thrown away that dumps couldn't hold it all. Our once beautiful planet was in serious trouble!

Water pollution (top left), smog (top right), damage to trees and plants from acid rain (above), and overflowing garbage dumps (left) had become serious problems by the late 1900s.

By the mid-1900s, people began to realize that pollution was affecting the Earth. Several large accidents made people even more aware of this. In 1969, a leak from an **offshore oil well** near Santa Barbara, California, poured tons of oil into the Pacific Ocean. In 1989, the *Exxon Valdez*, a huge ship carrying oil, crashed near Alaska. Again, oil spilled into the ocean. In

Workers trying to clean up the 1969 oil spill in Santa Barbara, California

both accidents, many animals and birds died from the pollution. People knew something needed to be done to help clean up our planet.

032699

The Birth of Earth Day

Among many others, there was one person who was very concerned about what was happening. In the 1960s, United States Senator Gaylord Nelson of Wisconsin worked hard to pass laws to protect the **environment**. He spoke to President John F. Kennedy

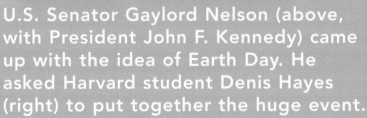

U.S. Senator Gaylord Nelson (above, with President John F. Kennedy) came up with the idea of Earth Day. He asked Harvard student Denis Hayes (right) to put together the huge event.

about his concerns. He gave speeches about taking better care of the Earth.

Senator Nelson wanted to get everyone, everywhere, involved. He thought of an idea: to set aside one special day to honor our planet. This day would be called Earth Day. He asked a talented young man named Denis Hayes to help organize this huge event.

To prepare for Earth Day, Senator Nelson asked people across the nation to join together. He wanted them to talk about ways people can take care of the environment. Some people agreed to teach classes. Others prepared speeches. Schools, towns, and cities planned special activities.

Earth Day was held on April 22, 1970. It was a great success. People marched in parades. At picnics and rallies, people made speeches about protecting the environment. Neighborhoods, towns, and cities held community clean-ups. Classes about caring for the environment were taught at schools and colleges.

The first Earth Day was an important beginning. After it was held, more and more people began joining **environmental groups**. Citizens began urging the U.S. government to work harder to protect the environment. In response, Congress passed stricter laws against air and water pollution.

By 1990, there had been many good changes. That year, to celebrate the twentieth anniversary of Earth Day, Denis Hayes organized a second Earth Day event. This time, he asked people from all over the world to participate.

Millions of people took part in the first International Earth Day, held in 1990.

On April 22, 1990, more
than 200 million people in 141
different countries celebrated
the first International Earth
Day. Children drew posters.
Volunteers picked up trash
and litter. Trees were planted.
People all over the world gave
speeches, sang, and marched
to show they cared about
the Earth.

The first two Earth Days
were so successful that people
decided to celebrate Earth Day

On Earth Day, now celebrated every year, people all over the world clean up trash, plant trees, and hold rallies to "save the Earth."

every year. They realized that it is important to take care of the planet every day.

Let's Keep it Clean!

Soon after the first Earth Day was celebrated in 1970, a special government **agency** was set up. This agency is called the U.S. Environmental Protection Agency (EPA). Its job is to make sure that people, businesses, and the government obey laws that

have been passed to help keep the Earth clean.

One of the EPA's concerns is pollution. Pollution affects the air we breathe. Even if air doesn't look dirty, it can still be full of harmful chemicals.

Car exhaust is a major cause of air pollution. Using cars powered by cleaner energy sources, such as electricity, could help reduce air pollution.

The main cause of air pollution is the burning of such **fossil fuels** as oil and coal. Cars, trucks, airplanes, factories, businesses, and most homes are powered by fossil fuels. When burned, fossil fuels release gases that can make the air unhealthy.

The gases released by the burning of fossil fuels are also making temperatures on Earth higher than they used to be. This problem is called global warming. No one knows what the exact effects of global warming will be.

Global warming is causing some of Earth's ice sheets to melt. As global sea levels rise, coastal flooding could occur in certain parts of the world.

Carpooling (above) or riding a bike to work (right) can help reduce air pollution.

If the Earth's climate changes too quickly, though, many plants and animals—including humans—could have problems surviving.

People can help keep the air clean—and help slow global warming—by buying cars that pollute less, sharing rides, and riding bikes. **Environmentalists** are trying to get people to stop relying on fossil fuels and switch to "clean" **energy** sources such as solar power and wind power.

Solar panels turn the sun's heat or light into electricity that can be used to power homes and businesses.

A young volunteer helps clean up a community lake.

Water pollution is another important environmental problem. Farmers use chemicals on their crops that seep through the ground and into the water. Factories pump wastes into rivers and streams. People dump trash into lakes and oceans. It takes a great effort by many people working together to stop pollution and help clean our water.

Our land is polluted as well. Farm chemicals can harm insects, birds, and people. Another problem is that there is too much trash thrown away. More and more land is being needed for dumps. People can

We can create less trash by recycling things instead of throwing them away.

help clean up the land by learning to reduce the amount of trash they throw away, reuse things, and recycle trash to make something new.

Let's Recycle!

Don't throw all your trash away! Let's recycle and make it into something new. Today, most communities recycle many different things, including glass, metal, cardboard, and plastic. Recycling helps our planet by putting less trash in the dumps. Just look at some of the things your trash can make!

A variety of items made from recycled plastic (above left) and a bubble wand made from a recycled coat hanger (above right)

RECYCLE   REUSE

REDUCE

Basics

SIMPLY THE BEST

MADE FROM
100% RECYCLED FIBERS

One World, One Voice

Earth Day has united people around the world who are interested in voicing their concerns about the Earth. Each year, more and more communities become part of Earth Day.

Cities in 184 different countries now hold Earth Day

Earth Day marchers in Hong Kong

events and programs. Displays
are set up to show better ways
of using energy and natural
resources. Children visit activity
booths to learn how to protect

Musicians entertaining an audience during an Earth Day celebration

the environment. Nature walks, music about nature, and wildlife art shows are included in the celebrations.

People who live near lakes and oceans help pick up litter

from the beaches. They organize boats to collect trash out of the water. Some people get together to plant grass and trees.

In the Philippines, many people participate in a famous bicycle ride. Their aim is to show others how bikes don't pollute the air. This encourages people to try other ways to get around besides using cars. Cars are among the worst causes of air pollution.

In Kenya, people show their concerns about deforestation— cutting down too many trees. Citizens join together to plant trees. Many trees have been planted in Kenya, as well as in other parts of the world.

All around the world, people hold neighborhood clean-ups. Neighbors pick up trash from streets, empty lots, and fields. People work together to help clean up the planet.

People cleaning up a neighborhood beach on Earth Day

Earth Day Every Day

On Earth Day, people pitch in to help clean up the Earth. We don't need to wait for April 22, however. It's important for us to take care of our planet every day.

Every person can do some-thing to help. You can throw trash away in a trashcan

Kids lining up to put their empty drink cans into a recycling bin

instead of tossing litter on the ground. You can buy one big bag of snacks instead of a lot of little bags that make more trash. You can help **conserve** natural resources

You can save water by turning the water off while brushing your teeth.

like water by turning the water off while you brush your teeth.

Earth is home for people, animals, and plants. Our actions help all of us share a

healthier planet. What we do today also affects future generations to come. Let's pitch in to help! Let's celebrate Earth Day every day.

To Find Out More

Here are some additional resources to help you learn more about Earth Day and environmental issues:

Books

Bonnet, Robert. **Environmental Science: 49 Science Fair Projects.** Tab Books, 1990.

Donald, Rhonda. **Water Pollution** (True Books). Children's Press, 2001.

Lowery, Lois. **Earth Day.** Carolrhoda Books, 1991.

Miller, Christina. **Air Alert: Rescuing the Earth's Atmosphere.** Atheneum, 1996.

Ross, Kathy. **Every Day Is Earth Day: A Craft Book.** Millbrook Press, 1995.

Stotsky, Sandra. **Pollution Problems and Solutions** (Ranger Rick's Naturescope). National Wildlife Federation, 1999.

Organizations and Online Sites

All Species Project

http://www.allspecies.org/

This site tells you how to hold "Earth Day in Your Neighborhood." You'll find such ideas as hosting a composting demonstration and performing a play. Check out other kids' projects and send in photos of your own.

DNR Kids Web

http://www.metrokc.gov/ dnr/kidsweb/

This site teaches kids about natural resources and how to conserve them. Explore wildlife habitats and learn where your trash goes when it leaves your home.

Earth Day

http://www.earthday. wilderness.org/

This site includes a message from Gaylord Nelson, the Founder of Earth Day. You can e-mail an Earth Day postcard to a friend, learn about migratory birds, and see a photo journal of an Arctic tour.

Earth Day Network

http://www.earthday.net/

Stay on top of the worldwide campaign to help our planet. Sign up to receive free e-mails of news from around the world.

Safe for Our Planet

http://www.safeforourplanet. com.au/

Play games, take the interactive tour, and find out about products that are safe for the Earth. Learn how to reduce, reuse, and recycle.

U.S. EPA Explorers Club

http://www.epa.gov/kids/

This site teaches all about such important things as the air quality index, a water treatment process, and saving endangered species. Play interactive games and create artwork as you explore this exciting site.

Important Words

agency department in the government

conserve to keep from becoming used up

energy power or heat used to make something work

environment surroundings of a living thing

environmental groups groups of people who are concerned about pollution and protecting our environment

environmentalists people who work to protect our environment

fossil fuels fuels, such as oil, coal, or natural gas, that are formed in the Earth from plant or animal remains

industries large businesses or factories, especially those that make products

natural resources valuable things found in nature such as water, trees, coal, or oil

offshore oil well oil well built in the ocean

Index

Meet the Author

Nancy I. Sanders grew up on a dairy farm in Everett, Pennsylvania. She has five older sisters and one older brother. Together, they spent many happy days playing outside. They swam in their pond on summer days. In the fall, they collected colorful leaves. Winter days found them playing "Fox and Geese" through trails they'd dug out of the snow. In the spring, they saw the baby calves.

Today, Nancy and her husband, Jeff, enjoy visiting the family farm with their sons, Dan and Ben. They fly from their home in California to visit relatives still living on the farm.